MW00977798

DENMARK ELEMENTARY
Media Center

# LAND OF LIBERTY

# AMERICA'S MIGHT

LYNN M. STONE

Rourke
Publishing LLC
Vero Beach, Florida 32964

© 2003 Rourke Publishing LLC

All rights reserved. No part of this book may be reproduced or utilized in any form or by any means, electronic or mechanical including photocopying, recording, or by any information storage and retrieval system without permission in writing from the publisher.

www.rourkepublishing.com

PHOTO CREDITS: All photos courtesy of Defense Visual Information Center.

Cover Photo: *A. U.S. Marine Corps AV-8B Harrier, wheels down, prepares to land on the flight deck of the U.S.S.* Tarawa.

Editor: Frank Sloan

Cover and page design by Nicola Stratford

**Library of Congress Cataloging-in-Publication Data**

Stone, Lynn. M
 America's might / Lynn M. Stone.
    p. cm. — (Land of liberty)
Includes bibliographical references and index

 ISBN 1-58952-311-3 (hardcover)
 1. United States—Armed Forces—Juvenile literature.

UA23 .S825 2002
355—dc21                                              2002004214

**Printed in the USA**

MP/W

# Table of Contents

America's Military ..................... 5

The Armed Forces .................... 6

Special Forces ........................ 7

Defending the Nation ................ 8

Keeping Peace ....................... 11

U.S. Air Force ....................... 12

U.S. Army ........................... 17

U.S. Marines ........................ 18

U.S. Navy ........................... 20

Glossary ............................ 23

Index ............................... 24

Further Reading/Websites to Visit   24

*F-16A Fighting Falcons armed with missiles are part of America's modern military might.*

# America's Military

One of America's early flags carried the words "Don't Tread on Me." It showed a rattlesnake. The message was that no one should attempt to mistreat or attack the United States. The message is the same today. By keeping her **military** mighty and modern, America can best protect herself and her interests.

America's military force is made up of her **armed** services. The armed services are the Air Force, Army, Marine Corps, and Navy.

# The Armed Forces

Each branch of service has its own armed forces. Those forces are made up of highly trained people using modern equipment and weapons. American weapons—tanks, guns, **missiles**, bombs, planes, ships—are second to none.

*Surface-to-air missile systems can be launched from the ground against flying targets.*

# Special Forces

Each branch also has small, highly skilled groups of Special Forces. Two of them are the Army's Green Berets and the Navy's SEALS.

*The Navy's Special Forces are known as the Sea-Air-Land SEALS. They undergo some of their training in water.*

# Defending the Nation

Throughout history, **hostile** nations and groups have sometimes been threats to the United States. The main job of the armed services, then and now, is to defend the nation. Sometimes the armed services are asked to do other jobs as well.

*A Sea Knight helicopter lifts a team of U.S. Marines from ground patrol training.*

*Training exercises, like this one with Army paratroopers in Alaska, prepare American soldiers for many kinds of operations.*

# Keeping Peace

American soldiers have been called upon to keep peace both at home and in other countries. They have helped people after warfare or natural disasters. American soldiers have helped people escape from war-torn cities. The American military services have also sent **advisors** to teach military skills to the soldiers of other countries.

# U.S. Air Force

The Air Force is one of three departments within the U.S. Department of Defense. (The other two are the departments of the Army and the Navy.) Like the other military services, the Air Force is under the command of the secretary of defense and the president of the United States.

*Air Force KC-135E Stratotanker refuels an F-111F fighter jet.*

*Two F-15E Eagles undergo last-minute ground checks before taking off.*

The Air Force handles most of the military operations in air and space. It has several kinds of aircraft. These range from attack and fighter jets to helicopters, bombers, and air tankers.

American fighter and attack aircraft are exceptionally fast and powerful. The F-15, for example, can fly nearly 2,000 miles (3,200 kilometers) per hour.

Long-range Air Force missiles (ICBMs) can reach targets 9,200 miles (14,720 kilometers) away.

*Equipped with missiles and practice bombs, Tomcat F-14A fighter jets fly in close formation.*

*The modern U.S. Army field forces have a place for women as well as men.*

# U.S. Army

The Army is the oldest branch of the military. It was begun in 1775 as the new United States fought against England.

The Army's main job is to conduct military operations on land. Many army soldiers are part of the **infantry**.

Like the other services, the Army has modern weapons. Some of them are **nuclear**. Nuclear weapons use nuclear energy. They are powerful and deadly.

# U.S. Marines

The proud American Marine Corps is within the Department of the Navy. However, it is not part of the Navy. It is a separate service.

*U.S. Marines roll ashore in an AAVP-7A1 amphibious assault vehicle.*

*A Marine recruit in the all-female 4th Battalion prepares to climb a cargo net to the top of a tower.*

The Marines are largely a highly trained ground force. They are often part of missions that require dangerous landings on beaches in wartime. Marines are trained and equipped to fight in every climate.

# U.S. Navy

The U.S. Navy's job is to fight an enemy at or near the sea. The Navy uses jet aircraft and modern warships as well as a variety of missiles.

Navy warships include aircraft carriers, battleships, cruisers, frigates, destroyers, and submarines.

*The U.S. Navy's nuclear-powered aircraft carrier* Abraham Lincoln *sails under cloudy skies.*

The U.S. Coast Guard acts under Navy orders in wartime or at the president's command.

For America's military, the job is on land, in the air, and at sea.

*Boatswain's mate directs an E-2C Hawkeye aircraft on the flight deck of the U.S.S.* Nimitz.

# Glossary

**advisor** (ad VIZE uhr) – one who offers advice, information, and teaching

**armed** (ARMD) – to be equipped with weapons

**hostile** (HOS tul) – referring to an enemy

**infantry** (IN fun tree) – an army's ground forces, foot soldiers

**military** (MILL uh tar ee) – referring to soldiers, armed forces, warfare

**missiles** (MISS uhlz) – objects that are sent to strike a set target

**nuclear** (NEW klee ur) – that which is powered by atomic energy, such as a nuclear bomb or aircraft carrier

# Index

Air Force   5, 12, 13
aircraft   13, 14, 20
armed services   5, 6, 8
Army   5, 12, 17
Coast Guard   22
Marine Corps   5, 18
Marines   19

missiles   6, 14, 20
Navy   5, 12, 20
nuclear weapons   17
SEALS   7
ships   6, 20
soldiers   11, 17
Special Forces   7

## Further Reading

Aaseng, Nathan. *Marine Corps in Action.* Enslow, 2001
Abramovitz, Melissa. *The U.S. Navy at War.* Capstone, 2001
Green, Michael. *U.S. Army Special Operations Forces.*
   Capstone, 2000

## Websites to Visit

Air Force Link Junior for Kids at http://www.af.mil/aflinkjr/jr.htm
U.S. Army at http://www.army.mil/
U.S. Marines at http://www.usmc.mil/
U.S. Navy at http://www.navy.mil/

## About the Author

Lynn Stone is the author of over 400 children's nonfiction books. He is a talented natural history photographer as well. Lynn, a former teacher, travels worldwide to photograph wildlife in its natural habitat.